Being Human

100 Quotes On Life, Love, And Compassion

Om Books International

First published in 2025

Om Books International

Corporate & Editorial Office
A-12, Sector 64, Noida 201 301
Uttar Pradesh, India
Phone: +91 120 477 4100
Email: editorial@ombooks.com
Website: www.ombooksinternational.com

Sales Office
107, Ansari Road, Darya Ganj,
New Delhi 110 002, India
Phone: +91 11 4000 9000
Email: sales@ombooks.com
Website: www.ombooks.com

ISBN: 978-93-63959-10-1

Printed in India

10 9 8 7 6 5 4 3 2 1

To...

From...

To be human is to be beautifully flawed.

Mitch Albom

Being human is a given. But keeping our humanity is a choice.

Anonymous

To err is
human;
to forgive,
divine.

Alexander Pope

The essence of being human is that one does not seek perfection.

George Orwell

To be human is to live in a world that is broken and has the potential for both joy and sorrow.

David Whyte

Being human means you will make mistakes. And you will make mistakes because failure is God's way of moving you in another direction.

Oprah Winfrey

We are
human
beings,
not human
doings.

Anonymous

The most important thing is to be whatever you are without shame.

Rod Steiger

The great blessing of humanity is our capacity to see the potential in others, and the willingness to do something about it.

Anonymous

To be human is
to be a collection
of contradictory
truths.

David Whyte

The purpose
of life is to be
defeated by greater
and greater things.

Rainer Maria Rilke

What makes us human is not our mind but our heart.

Anonymous

We are
all just
walking
each
other
home.

Ram Dass

TO BE HUMAN IS TO BE A STORYTELLER.

Karen Armstrong

It is the soul's duty to be loyal to its own desires.

Rebecca West

**We are not
human beings
having a
spiritual experience;
we are
spiritual beings
having a
human experience.**

Pierre Teilhard de Chardin

The most human thing we can do is comfort the afflicted and afflict the comfortable.

Clarence Darrow

To be human
is to love,
and to love
is to risk.

C.S. Lewis

Human beings have an inalienable right to invent themselves.

Germaine Greer

The beauty of being human is that we are all imperfect.

Anonymous

THE GREATEST
THING IN THE
WORLD IS TO
KNOW HOW
TO BELONG TO
ONESELF.

Michel de Montaigne

Humanity is
the virtue
of a woman,
generosity that
of a man.

Adam Smith

The human heart, at whatever age, opens only to the heart that opens in return.

Maria Edgeworth

Our humanity is a thing we have learned, and more from our **failures** than our success.

Anonymous

To be human is to need others.

Anonymous

Being human is not about being any one particular way; it is about being as life creates you–with your own particular strengths and weaknesses, gifts and challenges, quirks and oddities.

Kristin Neff

HUMANITY
IS THE ONLY
RELIGION WORTH
FOLLOWING.

Anonymous

THE REAL QUESTION
IS NOT WHETHER LIFE
EXISTS AFTER DEATH.
THE REAL QUESTION
IS WHETHER YOU ARE
ALIVE BEFORE DEATH.

Osho

To be human is to be aware of the passage of time.

Jorge Luis Borges

The best way to find yourself is to lose yourself in the service of others.

Mahatma Gandhi

The true meaning of life is to plant trees, under whose shade you do not expect to sit.

Nelson Henderson

Human beings are
works in progress
that mistakenly
think they're
finished.

Dan Gilbert

THE HUMAN SPIRIT MUST PREVAIL OVER TECHNOLOGY.

Albert Einstein

To be human is to have a collection of memories that tells you who you are and how you got there.

Rosecrans Baldwin

COMPASSION
IS THE CHIEF
LAW OF
HUMAN
EXISTENCE.

Fyodor Dostoevsky

To be human
is to be
perpetually
uncertain.

Lewis Thomas

HUMAN BEINGS CAN ALTER THEIR LIVES BY ALTERING THEIR ATTITUDES OF MIND.

William James

The most beautiful part of being human is the gift of being able to feel things deeply.

Anonymous

TO BE HUMAN
IS TO FIGHT FOR
THE GREATER
GOOD.

Anonymous

The best portion of a good man's life is his little, nameless, unremembered acts of kindness and of love.

William Wordsworth

Humanity
is a family,
a great
solidarity.

Auguste Comte

The human heart has hidden treasures, in secret kept, in silence sealed; the thoughts, the hopes, the dreams, the pleasures, whose charms were broken if revealed.

Charlotte Bronte

TO BE HUMAN
IS TO BE
A BRIDGE
BETWEEN
HEAVEN AND
EARTH.

Anonymous

The true sign of intelligence is not knowledge but imagination.

Albert Einstein

HUMANITY'S GREATEST ADVANCES ARE NOT IN ITS DISCOVERIES BUT IN HOW THOSE DISCOVERIES ARE APPLIED TO REDUCE INEQUITY.

Bill Gates

To be human is to cry for others.

Anonymous

**THE PURPOSE
OF HUMAN LIFE
IS TO SERVE,
AND TO SHOW
COMPASSION AND
THE WILL TO
HELP OTHERS.**

Albert Schweitzer

The human race has one really effective weapon, and that is laughter.

Mark Twain

To be human
is to
cherish the past,
to dream
of the future,
and to
live in the
moment.

Anonymous

What we do
for ourselves
dies with us.
What we do
for others and
the world
remains and is
immortal.

Albert Pike

The human heart is the first home of democracy.

Terry Tempest Williams

We are all of us stars, and we deserve to twinkle.

Marilyn Monroe

TO BE HUMAN
IS TO LIVE
WITH THE
CERTAINTY
OF THE
UNKNOWN.

Anonymous

OUR TASK MUST BE TO FREE OURSELVES BY WIDENING OUR CIRCLE OF COMPASSION TO EMBRACE ALL LIVING CREATURES AND THE WHOLE OF NATURE IN ITS BEAUTY.

Albert Einstein

The good life is one inspired by love and guided by knowledge.

Bertrand Russell

To be human is to endure the pain and embrace the joy.

Anonymous

HUMANITY'S TRUE MORAL TEST, ITS FUNDAMENTAL TEST, CONSISTS OF ITS ATTITUDE TOWARDS THOSE WHO ARE AT ITS MERCY: ANIMALS.

Milan Kundera

The human spirit
is **stronger** than
anything that can
happen to it.

C.C. Scott

To be human is to wonder at the beauty and the mystery of **existence**.

Anonymous

THE ULTIMATE MEASURE OF A MAN IS NOT WHERE HE STANDS IN MOMENTS OF COMFORT, BUT WHERE HE STANDS AT TIMES OF CHALLENGE AND CONTROVERSY.

Martin Luther King Jr.

We are what we repeatedly do. Excellence, then, is not an act, but a habit.

Aristotle

TO BE HUMAN IS TO LIVE ON THE EDGE OF THE WORLD, AND TO CREATE OUR OWN MAP.

Anonymous

I AM A HUMAN BEING, NOTHING HUMAN CAN BE ALIEN TO ME.

Terence

THE HUMAN RACE IS CHALLENGED MORE THAN EVER BEFORE TO DEMONSTRATE OUR MASTERY, NOT OVER NATURE BUT OF OURSELVES.

Rachel Carson

To be human is to love and be loved.

Anonymous

Humanity is
not thinking
less of
yourself,
but thinking
of yourself
less.

C.S. Lewis

To be human is to rise above our limitations.

Anonymous

We must learn to live together as brothers or perish together as fools.

Martin Luther King Jr.

THE HUMAN MIND IS OUR FUNDAMENTAL RESOURCE.

John F. Kennedy

To be human is to forgive others and ourselves.

Anonymous

BEING HUMAN IS BEING MADE IN THE IMAGE OF GOD.

John Piper

Humanity is about being able to accept the **fragile** and **vulnerable** nature of being human.

Anonymous

TO BE HUMAN IS TO EXPERIENCE A FULL SPECTRUM OF EMOTIONS.

Anonymous

We are human precisely because we can **adapt** to situations that are outside our original nature.

Yuval Noah Harari

The more I see
of humanity, the
more I marvel
at what I don't
understand.

Mark Twain

To be human is to be imperfect and vulnerable.

Anonymous

The greatness of humanity is not in being human, but in being humane.

Mahatma Gandhi

If there is meaning in life at all, then there must be meaning in **suffering**.

Viktor E. Frankl

Every human
is an artist.
The dream of
your life is
to make
beautiful art.

Don Miguel Ruiz

To be human
is to be
broken and
broken is its
own kind of
beautiful.

Robert M. Drake

A HUMAN BEING IS A BEING WHO IS CONSTANTLY 'UNDER CONSTRUCTION,' BUT ALSO, IN A PARALLEL FASHION, ALWAYS IN A STATE OF CONSTANT DESTRUCTION.

José Saramago

We think too much and feel too little. More than machinery, we need humanity.

Charlie Chaplin

TO BE
HUMAN
IS TO BE A
CREATOR OF YOUR
OWN DESTINY.

Anonymous

It is not what we get.
But who we become,
what we contribute...
that gives meaning to
our lives.

Tony Robbins

The most authentic thing about us is our capacity to create, to overcome, to endure, to transform, to love, and to be greater than our suffering.

Ben Okri

The function of freedom is to free someone else.

Toni Morrison

The human condition is a good one in that no one is unhappy except by their own fault.

Seneca

Man is the only
creature who refuses to
be what he is.

Albert Camus

To live is the rarest thing in the world. Most people exist, that is all.

Oscar Wilde

It is not our differences that divide us. It is our inability to recognize, accept, and celebrate those differences.

Audre Lorde

To be human is to have the courage to be vulnerable.

Anonymous

Humanity is
about being able
to see the world
through a lens of
possibility.

Anonymous

To be human is to have the courage to chase your dreams.

Anonymous

Humanity is about being able to see the world as a place of endless opportunities for growth and change.

Anonymous

To be human is to have the courage to love deeply and without reservation.

Anonymous

Being human is a matter of perspective, not biology.

Anonymous

**The only thing
that makes
life possible
is permanent,
intolerable
uncertainty:
not knowing
what comes next.**

Ursula K. Le Guin

The most beautiful thing about being human is that we are all different, yet the same.

Anonymous

To be human
is to embrace
both the light
and the dark
within us.

Anonymous

The greatness of being human lies in our capacity for **growth** and **change**.

Steve Jobs